The Fine Art of Cutting and Screening:
Improve Your Basketball Team by Improving Execution of the Offensive Building Blocks

Kevin Sivils

A Southern Family Publishing

KCS Basketball Enterprises, LLC
Katy, Texas

The Fine Art of Cutting and Screening:
Improve Your Basketball Team by Improving Execution of the Offensive Building Blocks

Copyright 2012 Kevin Sivils
All Rights Reserved
ISBN: 1475183100
ISBN-13: 978-1475183108

Photography by Jeremy Yutzy of Yutzy Photography unless otherwise indicated.

Photography by Maddy Copello

No part of this publication may be reproduced, stored in a retrieval system, or transmitted, in any form by any means, electronic, mechanical, photocopying, recording or otherwise, without written permission from the author.

Published by *A Southern Family Publishing*

A Division of KCS Basketball Enterprises, LLC

www.kcsbasketball.com

CONTENTS

Basic Offensive Building Blocks of Every Effective Offense	1
Basic Principles for Cutting to be Effective	5
Basic Principles of Cutting	11
Basics of Setting a Screen	15
The Basic Screens	19
Basics of Using a Screen	23
Putting It All Together	27
Setting and Using on the Ball Screens	31
Simple Drills to Teach Screening and Cutting	35
Lagniappe - Something Extra	47
About the Author	63
To Contact the Author	65

Basic Offensive Building Blocks of Every Effective Offense

Regardless of whether or not the system of offense used is a continuity, set play or a motion style of offense, every offensive system has basic building blocks essential to the success of the offense and the team running the offense. These basic building blocks include:

- The TEAM Concept
- Mastery and Execution of Fundamentals
- Spacing
- Ball Movement (passing and dribble penetration)
- Player Movement (cutting)
- Screening
- Combination of Offensive Building Blocks (timing and execution)
- Offensive Rebounding

The TEAM Concept

Basketball is a team sport. The interaction of the five players on the court is what makes it fun and so exciting to watch. Nothing spoils good basketball like a selfish player who refuses to play within the team concept or a group of individuals masquerading as a team.

The combined efforts of each member of the roster, when fully meshed as a team unit, produce a synergy capable of amazing things. Few things are as miserable or as dysfunctional as a group of selfish individuals posing as a team. In fact, the most important concept in the entire sport of basketball is the TEAM concept!

A real TEAM produces a sum that is greater than the numerical sum of the values of the players! Not only is this true, but TEAMS have more fun, are able to deal with adversity in a more positive manner, accept challenges, are more fun to watch and a significantly more positive experience for each individual who is part of this special group known as a TEAM!

Mastery and Execution of Fundamentals

When an offense does not functional properly it is due to one of three reasons. The first is beyond the control of a team and is due to the opponent. Namely, the opponent is playing good defense and disrupting the execution of the offense. The second reason is the failure of the players to play within a team concepts, to cooperate with each other for the benefit of the team.

The most common reason any offense breaks down in execution is the failure of the players to properly execute the basic fundamentals of the game at game speed under game conditions. The offense is not broken, the fundamentals are. Failure on the part of the coach to insist upon mastery and execution of fundamentals will lead to failure to execute against any opponent who can play average defense.

Spacing

Spacing is offense and offense is spacing. Like many things, it sounds too simple when first heard, but the adage is true.

Good offense, regardless of what offense is being run, requires proper spacing. Proper spacing alone will provide the following positive benefits for any offense:

- Gaps in the defense to drive
- Spacing will stretch the defense making it more difficult to give help
- Increasing the difficulty in providing help forces the defense to close to the ball too rapidly when recovering, creating driving opportunities that often result in drawing a foul and an excellent scoring opportunity.
- Proper spacing increases the ease with which the offense can move the ball by passing due to the increased difficulty the defense has in denying passes.
- Proper spacing ensures floor balance and better offensive rebounding opportunities.

What is good spacing? Players should be 15-18 feet apart and play behind the NBA three-point line. These two principles will stretch the defense optimally and ensure that college and high school three point shots, when open and taken, are behind the appropriate arc for that level of competition.

Another aspect of proper spacing is balancing the floor in terms of the number of players on one side of the floor. The ideal spacing formation is four players on the perimeter, even if one or more is a post player, and one player in the post, either high or low.

Let's examine three popular formations and note how these rules apply. One of the most common forms of motion offense is the 4-out-1-in, which is also the preferred set for the new Dribble Drive Motion. The popular Flex offense when spaced properly also assumes a 4-out-1-in alignment. Finally the famed UCLA High Post offense features a 4-out-1-in alignment except the post player is in the high post.

The 4-out-1-in alignment allows for excellent floor balance for offensive rebounding, insuring a minimum of two rebounders on the weak side of the court, the side 80% of rebounds will come out on, as well as an organized starting point to begin transition defense.

Ball Movement

After proper spacing, moving the ball is the next essential element of good offense. Offenses that rely on one-on-one player, pick and roll action, etc, are fine so long as the individual player is significantly better than the defender assigned to stop that player. Quality defensive teams will help a defender guard the great offensive player. Help defense tries to overload the ball side of the court to prevent the offense from having success. This can be a significant advantage for the defense since, depending on the offensive alignment, the defense can have a 5-on-3 or even a 5-on-2 numerical advantage.

One of the keys to eliminating the defense's numerical advantage is to move the ball from one side of the court to the other, forcing the defense to move from ball side to help side and back to ball side in a short period of time. This not only will eliminate the numerical advantage from help positioning, but can force the defense into making mistakes due to the constant repositioning.

Player Movement

Simply moving the ball can create scoring opportunities. Moving players makes the offense even more effective as it forces the defense to adjust its help side positioning, ball side positioning and increases the possibility of the defense making a mistake. A moving player is always more difficult to defend than a stationary player.

Screening

Spacing, moving the ball and moving people are a great start to a good offense. Adding screening and cutting off screens into the mix and the offense becomes difficult to defend.

Keys to successful screening and cutting are simple but key. These include:

- Screening a defender and not space.
- Waiting for the screen to be set.
- Using a v-cut with proper change of pace to set up and use the screen.
- Setting the screen at the correct angle.
- Reading the defender's method of fighting off the screen correctly and then selecting the correct cut.

Combination of Offensive Building Blocks

Each offensive building block by itself can be an effective means of generating offensive opportunities. When combined in an organized and well thought out manner, effective offense is created. Combining screening and cutting with ball movement and a penetration game creates multiple challenges for even the best defensive team.

Offensive Rebounding

The final component of good offense is an organized and effective approach to obtaining offensive rebounds, regardless of either a motion offense or some type of set play or continuity is used. A key requirement of each to be successful is some kind of organized plan to obtain a significant number of offensive rebounds

All strategies for offensive rebounding have several key components. One is the approach is organized and systematic and to be applied each time the offense generates a field goal attempt. The other is a systematic attempt to overload the weak, or help, side of the court in an effort to obtain a numerical advantage over the defense when attacking the boards. The third component is an organized transition from offense to rebounding to defensive transition.

Most common approaches send three offensive rebounders to the boards with two players retreating to stop any fast break attempts by the opponent. A more aggressive approach is to send four offensive rebounders to the boards with the shooter moving to the top of the key for a three-point attempt following an offensive rebound.

Regardless of the approach used, it is important to emphasize the need to hit the offensive glass. Remember, players don't do what coaches teach, they always do what is emphasized!

Basic Principles for Cutting to be Effective

Use Hand Targets to Communicate With the Passer

Passing requires communication between the player in possession of the ball and the player who desires to receive the ball. Verbal communication can be misunderstood or not heard during the chaos of a game. Visual signals with hands cannot be misunderstood and for this reason is a more effective method of communicating a cutter's intent to the passer.

Three basic hand signals must be learned by all players, allowing the cutter/shooter to communicate intent and the passer to anticipate where to pass the ball away from the defense. The first is an extended open hand, indicating the direction away from the goal the cutter/shooter intends to cut towards.

The second hand signal is the clinched fist, indicating the shooter/cutter intends to cut "backdoor," in the direction of the goal. This cut is used when the defense is applying intense overplay denial defense, a common tactic used against excellent 3-point shooters in the desire to prevent the shooter from receiving the ball beyond the 3-point line.

The third and final hand signal is used to indicate the shooter is open and ready to shoot upon receiving the ball. This signal is indicated by the shooter having hands in the shooting pocket, knees bent ready to shoot and being squared up to the goal. The shooter needs only to catch the pass in order to shoot if the passer makes an accurate pass directly into the shooting pocket.

Directional Hand Target   **Backdoor Hand Target**   **Ready to Shoot Target**

Pass Away From the Defense

Turnovers due to intercepted passes are usually a result of passing the ball to a teammate. Sounds silly, but it is true. Unless the teammate is wide open for a shot, the ball should never be passed directly to the teammate. Instead, the ball must be passed away from the defense. This includes both the defender guarding the passer (**Photograph A**) and the cutter (**Photograph B**).

Photograph A by Maddy Copello

Photograph B by Maddy Copello

Shorten the pass

Not only must the passer pass the ball away from the defense using a frozen rope, the cutter/shooter must "shorten the pass" by stepping in the direction of the oncoming pass to meet the ball. This decreases the chances of the defense intercepting the pass and increases the likelihood of a foul on an aggressive denial defender.

This technique also allows a shooter who is coming off a screen or who has simply made a flash cut to set up his/her footwork to catch the ball, face-up, get on balance and in a smooth continuous motion shoot the ball.

Players must be trained to create this habit. The technique utilizes a start step, the same start step a player uses to pass a ball, execute a direct drive or crossover step or to jump stop. The player steps towards the ball with an aggressive, long, low start step, propelling the player towards the ball.

Pass the Ball Where it Can Be Caught

It is not enough to pass the ball away from the defense. The ball has to be passed to the receiver in a location the receiver can safely catch the ball. Passing the ball where it can be caught entails two different concepts. The first concerns the receiver physically being able to the catch the ball. The second involves court and defender location.

Every player has different a different ability level when it comes to catching a basketball. Some players can pull the ball in safely if they can simply touch the ball with their fingertips. Others require the ball to arrive at a location more central to their chest area. Some players are able to move to the ball with ease in order to catch a pass while others are not. The passer must know the level of ability to receive a pass of every player on the team.

Passing the ball simply because the offense requires the ball to go to a specific player in the play or a specific location on the court for the play to continue is not license to simply force a pass into the offensive player occupying that position or location.

The passer must be aware of the surrounding defensive players and factor this into the equation of making the decision to pass or not. Most experienced post players are adept at catching a lob pass when fronted by a defender. This does not mean the ball should be just lobbed in.

The defense may have a help side defender located directly behind the post in order to draw a charge when the pass is made. Other teams may anticipate well and bait teams into making a lob pass allowing the defense to either deflect the pass away and create a steal or draw a charge off the post player. Passers must factor in all of these variables in deciding whether or not to make a pass.

Move to Catch the Pass

Not only must the passer pass the ball away from the defense using a frozen rope, the cutter/shooter must "shorten the pass" by stepping in the direction of the oncoming pass to meet the ball. This decreases the chances of the defense intercepting the pass and increases the likelihood of a foul on an aggressive denial defender.

This technique also allows a shooter who is coming off a screen or who has simply made a flash cut to set up his/her footwork to catch the ball, face-up, get on balance and in a smooth continuous motion shoot the ball.

Players must be trained to create this habit. The technique utilizes a start step, the same start step a player uses to pass a ball, execute a direct drive or crossover step or to jump stop. The player steps towards the ball with an aggressive, long, low start step, propelling the player towards the ball.

Catch the Ball With Your Eyes

Coaches tell players to keep their eye on the ball and with good reason. Many mishandled passes are a result of a player taking his eyes off the ball before catching it. Telling a player to catch the ball with his eyes is a better concept to communicate to a player. This terminology tells the player exactly how long the player's vision must be maintained on the ball and aids the player in concentrating completely on the ball until it has been caught.

In other words, all the way into the player's hands, making the verbal cue to "catch the ball with your eyes" an excellent coaching prompt to improve receiving and catching a pass, either when wide open or in defensive traffic.

Making the Backdoor Pass

From an artistic standpoint, there are few plays in the game of basketball more pleasing to the eye than a perfectly executed play. On the surface, this is a seemingly simple play, which is perhaps why it is so appealing to the fan who witnesses the perfectly executed backdoor play.

Yet, if this play is so "easy" why do so many pressure defenses, which are vulnerable to the backdoor pass, played by so many teams? The answer is also simple, the backdoor pass and cut is not as easy to execute as it seems! Executing the backdoor cut is addressed in the chapter on cutting but this point needs to be made clear so the manner in which the backdoor pass must be made is understandable.

It is not enough to beat the defender backdoor, the cutter must be able to receive the ball and score. Herein lies the problem! Most backdoor passes do indeed beat the defender, but the pass is not thrown in such a way the cutter can receive the ball or do something positive with the ball after receiving it. The main issue is one of space, having an area allowing room to both catch the ball and then make a pass or score a basket. Most passers fail to create the needed space for the cutter by passing the ball at a bad angle. The type of pass used can also be problematic.

Direct chest passes or overhead passes can be difficult for the cutter to catch due to the velocity of the ball and the angle of the pass. The solution to both problems is to only pass the ball in a manner that insures the needed space is provided and the ball can be caught by the cutter! To successfully make a backdoor pass every time the play is attempted, the passer needs only to pass the ball directly down the lane line, perpendicular to the baseline, using a bounce pass.

If necessary, the passer should drive to the lane line extended to make the pass. By using this technique, the cutter will obtain possession of the ball just outside of the lane, ensuring sufficient space is available to catch the ball and have sufficient area and space to shoot the ball.

The use of the bounce pass, while quick, lessens the velocity of the ball sufficiently so the ball can be handled by the cutter. This is a simple concept to demonstrate and easy for players to learn. Adding this to a player's repertoire will make for a much better passer!

Basic Principles of Cutting

Make Angles, Not Curves When Cutting

Defenders have an easier time dealing with cutters who use "curves" rather than "angles" when making a cut. In both of the diagrams shown below, the defender does not have to cover as much ground defensively or absorb a change in pace.

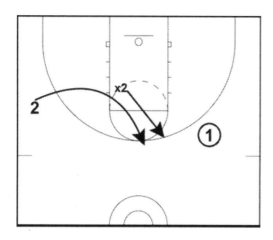 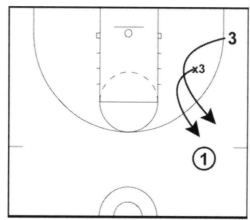

By making a v-cut, using an angle and not a curve when cutting, the cutter forces the defense to cover more ground defensively and absorb the sudden change in direction when the second half of the v-cut is made. The diagrams below show how much more ground the defender must cover and keep in mind the change of pace makes the change of direction more difficult to defend.

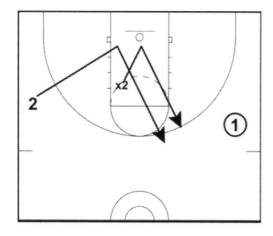 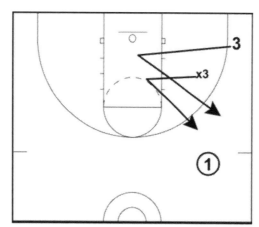

Go In Slow, Come Out Fast!

V-cuts require not only the use of an angle and not a curve, but a change of pace as well. The cutter moves into the v-cut slowly, changes direction and accelerates to full speed as quickly as possible. The change of pace combined with the angle and change of direction makes the cutter much more difficult for the individual defensive player to defend.

Plant the Opposite Foot to Cut

If a cutter desires to cut to his or her right, the cutter must plant the foot opposite the intended direction the player intends to cut to, in this case the left foot is the foot the player pants and pushes off with.

Use a "Straight Line" When Possible

The shortest distance between two points is a straight line. Whenever possible, cutters should move in straight lines, making life as difficult as possible for the defender. While this is not always possible, cutters should apply this concept as much as possible. Curved cuts should be made as straight as possible unless screens are being set such as would happen in a double or triple staggered screen.

Raise Hands Coming Out of a V-cut

Whether the cutter is cutting or using a screen when coming out of a v-cut, the cutter must raise his or her hands either to communicate the direction the cutter is planning to move in or to be ready to receive a pass should the cutter be open.

Know How to "Finish" a Complete Cut

The lane area around the goal is valuable real estate in the game of basketball. The defense will do everything it can to congest this space, post players struggle to carve out as much space as possible and point guards love to have the room to drive into this area.

Cutters often clog this valuable court space by cutting into the area needlessly. Cutters must learn to identify when a cut is "finished." If the cutter has a chance to be open for a pass or plays in an offense that requires pulling a defender through the lane as deeply as possible to create space elsewhere in the offense, the cutter should make a basket cut.

The diagram below to the left depicts a basket cut. The cutter has continued the cut all the way to the rim and then cut to an open space on the court, clearing the lane for other offensive players to have an opportunity to operate.

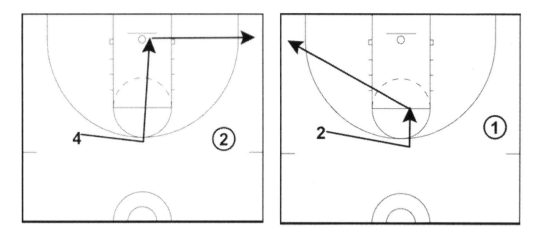

The diagram to above and to the right depicts a cutter who has "broken off" the cut just below the foul line, leaving the lane area open. Notice the cutter is now in line with the ball and any potential cutter in the help side area of the court. This is the tactic screeners should use to set up down screens.

Basics of Setting a Screen

Sett the Screen Up - Communicate

The first step in the screening process is to set the screen up. This involves the screener, who must communicate to the cutter a screen is going to be set, and the cutter, who must receive the communication from the screener and recognize a screen is going to be set for him or her. The screener uses both hands to signal to the cutter that a screen is going to be set.

The Fine Art of Cutting and Screening

Set a Legal Screen

Once the screener and cutter have communicated to work together, the screener must set a legal screen avoiding committing a foul. This requires the screener to set the screen a legal distance from the defender being screened. In the case of any screen where the defender can see the screen coming, such as a down screen, the screener can make contact with the defender. On a blind screen, such as a back screen, the screener must give the defender one step to avoid having a foul called.

The screener sets the screen by executing a jump stop, protecting sensitive areas with both hands and remaining completely still. An ideal legal screen will be one where the screener's head is level or below that of the defender, the knees are slightly bent and the legs slightly wider than hip width apart. Once the screener has stopped to set the screen, it is up to the cutter to utilize the screen to get open. The screener must be ready to read the defender and adjust the screen angle and to be a second cutter.

Screen a Man and Not Space

Effective screens impede the progress of the defender. This requires contact to be made between the screener and the defender, hence the phrase "screen a man and not space." The photograph below shows the screener has "buried" the defender" with legal contact, established a wide base with knees bent and her head is level with that of the defender. The cutter has made contact with the screener and is communicating with a hand target to the passer.

In the photograph below the cutter has not waited for the screen to be set and the screener has not "screened a man and not space." There is a noticeable gap between the defender and the screener, allowing the defender to continue playing defense unimpeded.

Be a Second Cutter

The screener is now a second cutter.

The Fine Art of Cutting and Screening

After setting a screen and holding position until the cutter has cleared the screen, the screener executes a rear turn (pivot), shows his or her numbers to the ball and reads the defense. Often the screener and not the cutter will be open following a screen and cut. The screener may have to step towards the ball to receive a pass or cut to the goal as shown in the diagrams below.

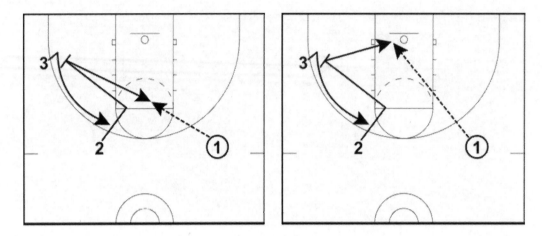

The Basic Screens

Down Screen

Down Screen

Off all the basic offensive building blocks, the down screen is one of the most simple to implement. In the diagram above, #3 cuts to the line between the offensive player with the ball and the player to be screened for. #3 motions to #2 that he/she is going to screen for #2. #2 waits for the screen to be set. #3 sets a legal screen, making contact with the defender of #2, not the empty space, and remains stationary. #2 waits until the screen has been set, executes a v-cut to set the defender into the screen and rubs shoulders with the screener when coming off the screen. #2 must have hands up ready to receive the pass, face-up, look under the net and possibly shoot.

Flare Screen

Flare Screen

The flare screen is utilized to get players open on the perimeter wings. The screener is positioned on the wing, below the intended cutter. #3 signals to #2 a flare screen will be set. #3 must leave one step between the defender and the screen so a foul will not be called. #3's back must be facing the corner to establish the correct angle for the screen. #2 must v-cut to set the screen, rub shoulders with the screener and face the basket with hands ready to catch and knees bent ready to shoot.

Pin Screen

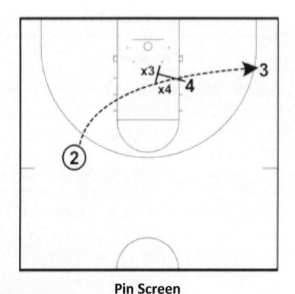

Pin Screen

The pin screen is an effective tool to create a large amount space for the shooter. The pin screen is particularly effective against teams who play excellent help side defense, positioning help defenders guarding perimeter players two or more passes away from the ball in the lane area to congest the lane and help defend the offensive low post (See the diagram). In the example shown #4 "pins" #3's defender, X3, into the lane, allowing a quick skip pass to #3 create an open 3-point shot. #4 can act as a second cutter by sealing X3 in the lane and posting up for a post entry pass from #3 if X4 closes-out to prevent the 3-point shot attempt.

Re-Screen

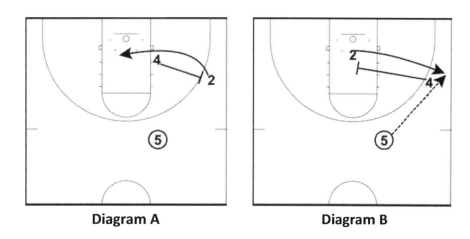

Diagram A   Diagram B

Re-screening is an excellent tactic to create shots. Multiple, successive screens is difficult to defend. There are multiple ways to re-screen a defender. In **Diagram A** #4 sets a back screen for #2. After shaping up to be a second cutter, #4 sets a pin screen for #2 who did not receive a pass on the back door cut. After pin screening for #2, #4 should seal and post if #2 does not have a good 3-point shot opportunity (**Diagram B**).

Common combinations for re-screen opportunities include down screen followed by a flare screen, flare screen followed by a down screen and a pin screen followed by a back screen.

The Fine Art of Cutting and Screening

Set and Use Correct Screen Angles

In addition to screening a man and not space, the proper angle must be set for the screen to be effective. The cutter also has a significant role to play in the process, setting the screen up, waiting for the screen to be set, reading the defender's reaction to the screen and accelerating out of the second half of the v-cut. Each type of screen and cut combination has a required screen angle that must be used in order for the screen to be effective. These required screening angles are specific to the type of screen as listed below:

- Down Screen – back to ball – **Diagram A**
- Flare Screen – back to corner – **Diagram B**
- Back Screen – back to basket – **Diagram C**
- Pin Screen – back to sideline – **Diagram D**

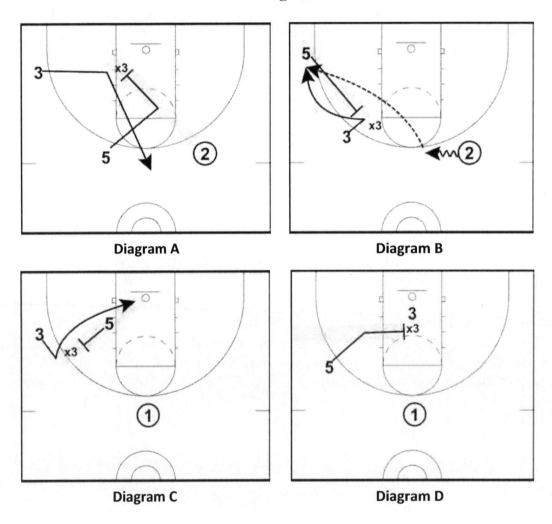

Diagram A Diagram B

Diagram C Diagram D

Basics of Using a Screen

Setting the Screen Up - Communication

The first step in the screening process is to set the screen up. This involves the screener, who must communicate to the cutter a screen is going to be set, and the cutter, who must receive the communication from the screener and recognize a screen is going to be set for him or her.

In the photograph on the left, the screener, Number 11, is communicating to the cutter, Number 12, with two hands raised above her shoulders with her palms facing towards the rear. Number 11 will motion with both hands in the direction she plans to set the screen and have Number 12 cut towards. Visual communication is silent and can at times allow the offense to surprise an unsuspecting defensive player with a screen.

In the photograph above and to the right, Number 12 has recognized the screen was going to be set, moved towards the lane to set up the second half of her v-cut, and waited for Number 12 to actually set the screen.

Wait, Wait, Wait

After recognizing a screen is going to be set, the cutter must execute the first half of a v-cut to establish the proper cutting angle to come off the screen and to draw the defender closer to the cutter, making the defender easier to screen. In the diagram below to the left, the screener has set the screen at a reasonably good angle for a down screen in relation to the location of the ball. The cutter, #3, cuts without waiting or using a v-cut, allowing the defender X3 to easily avoid the screen.

In the diagram below to the right, #3 cuts to the correct location and WAITS for the screen to be set. The defender, X3, will either remain stationary allowing the screener to establish the screen, or move closer to #3 in an effort to defend the cutter. The key to the screener and cutter being able to establish a good, solid, legal screen is for the cutter to execute the first half of the v-cut (go in slow, come out fast) and wait, wait, wait for the screener to set the screen.

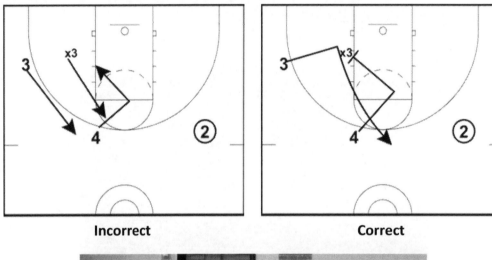

Incorrect **Correct**

The cutter did not wait for the screen to be set. The defender will easily avoid the screen and successfully defend the cutter.

Basics of Using a Screen

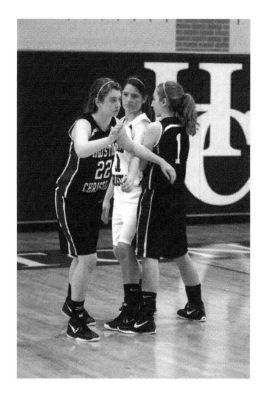

In the photograph to the left, the cutter, Number 22, recognized the screener, Number 1, was going to set a down screen. Number 22 moved in slowly to set the defender up to be screened.

Number 1 was able to screen a man and not space because in this example, Number 22, WAITED for the screen to be set. This allowed the screener to set a legal down screen with contact on the defender.

Note that Number 22 has made physical contact with the screener and is communicating the direction she intends to cut to with the appropriate hand signal to the player in possession of the ball.

Make Contact with the Screener

Good defenders fight through screens. They will move into the cutter before the screen is set, chase the outside hip and step over the screen, even if the cutter and screener have done everything correctly. This makes it essential that the cutter make physical contact with the screener and the more the better. In the photograph below the cutter has made shoulder-to-shoulder contact with the screener. Note how close the cutter's hip is to that of the screener. Very little room exists for the defender to slip, or fight, through.

The cut would be perfect if the cutter, Number 12, had come off the screen with her outside hand raised as a target to communicate the direction she intended to cut or to receive a pass for a shot if she was immediately open.

Have Your Hands Ready

The instant a cutter begins to clear a screen the cutter must have a minimum of one hand ready to either indicate the direction of the cut the cutter will execute. As quickly as possible the cutter must bring a second hand into a ready position to catch any pass made to the cutter.

Putting It All Together

"Reading" for Cuts

Unless the team is using a set play or a continuity offense with no flexibility, it makes little sense to set a specific screen all the time when running an offense. It is much more productive to set a specific screen based on the players engaged in the screening and cutting, court location and the ball location.

For example, it makes for sense for a non-shooter to screen for a shooter, a post player to set a flare screen for a 3-point shooter and for a down screen to be set for a player who likes to curl cut into the lane and draw a foul while scoring. It takes time and knowledge of teammates to read what screens to set, where to set them and when to set them.

Some times the screen being set by the screener is not to set the cutter up, but to obtain an open shot or good position to receive the ball. For example, a post player setting a pin screen for a perimeter player who is in the lane. The post player will be in excellent position after the screen to seal and receive a pass from the perimeter player who took advantage of the pin screen.

The manner in which the defense plays a screen can also determine the type of screen and cut to be used. For example, if the defense chases on a down screen, the cutter should curl cut into the lane (**Photograph Reading Cuts-A**). If the defense slips under the screen on a down screen the screener should change the angle to a pin screen and the cutter should fade cut behind the readjusted screen (**Photographs Reading Cuts-B and Reading Cuts-C**). In **Photograph Reading Cuts-D,** the screener has taken advantage of the manner in which the defense played the screen and cut and has posted up.

The Fine Art of Cutting and Screening

Reading Cuts-A

Reading Cuts-B

Reading Cuts-C

Reading Cuts-D

Putting It All Together

In the diagram above and to the left the defender has started to cheat over the screen as the cutter utilizes the screen. In a continuity or set play this can be problematic. With motion offense the cutter can wrap around the screen and make a curl cut, using the front, side and back of the screener to delay the defender.

In the above right diagram the defender has cheated completely over the down screen to prevent a curl cut, pop up cut or pop out cut. The screener reads the defense and readjusts the angle of the screen from a down screen to a back screen. The cutter now executes a back cut.

The above left diagram shows the defender fighting over a flare screen quickly. In the next diagram the screener is depicted setting a re-screen on the defender. This tactic is effective for nearly any screening situation. Defenders can often fight over one screen successfully. Two successive screens are make fighting over the second screen much more difficult, particularly as the game progresses.

The Fine Art of Cutting and Screening

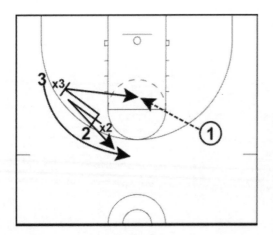 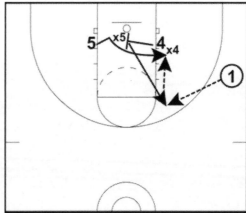

Some teams switch all screens on defense. This is where developing the habit of the screener being a second cutter becomes critical. All switches can be defeated by the use of the second cutter. The diagram above to the left depicts a perimeter screen being set and the screener receiving the pass as a second cutter. The diagram to the right above depicts setting up a high low pas by having the screener cut into the high post on the switch while the cutter seals the defender, X4, out of the lane for the high low pass.

Setting and Using on the Ball Screens

While always popular in the NBA, the on the ball screen, or ball screen for short, is enjoying a resurgence in the college and high school game. The most basic form of the pick and roll as the ball screen is often called is shown in the two diagrams below. In the diagram on the left the ball handler drives all the way to the goal for a lay-up and the screener has "rolled" and created space for the penetrating ball handler while obtaining good offensive rebounding position.

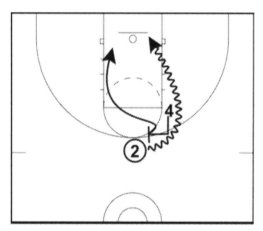 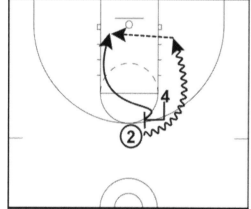

In the above right diagram it appears the defense has forced the ball handler wide or prevented the ball handler from attacking the rim. The ball handler has created space for a pass to the screener who has rolled up the lane. By staying well spaced, the ball handler prevents one defender from covering the two offensive players involved.

These two simple examples are an excellent way to teach the basics of a good on ball screen and the following "roll action." These principles include:

- The screener communicates a screen will be set prior to setting the screen.
- Setting the screen square to the ball handler (at a 90 degree angle).
- Screening a man and not space if legal.
- The cutter rubs shoulders with the screener when using the screen.
- The screener rolls to an appropriate open space on the court.
- Both the screener and the ball handler maintain proper spacing.

The Fine Art of Cutting and Screening

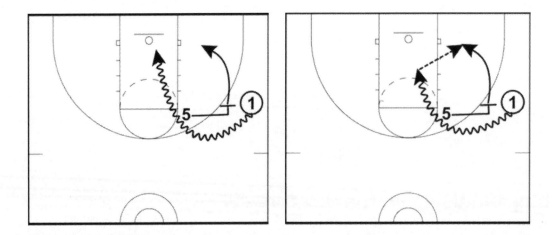

The on the ball screen is perhaps more effective when utilized on the wing as it allows for the offense to involve multiple players following the setting and the use of the screen. The diagram above and to the left depicts a screen and roll where the ball handler drives to the rim for a lay-up. The diagram above and to the right depicts a similar scenario but the ball handler passes to the screener who has "rolled" to an open space on the court for an open shot.

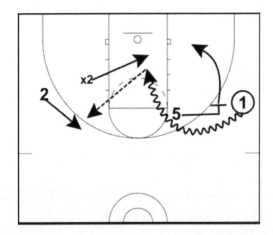

In this example, shown above, the ball handler has forced the defense to rotate off a 3-point shooter on the opposite wing by penetrating the lane. The shooter rotates back to an open area on the ball handler's middle penetration and prepares to receive a pass for a shot attempt or a penetrating drive into the lane. The ball handler must clear the lane after the pass to create space for additional offensive opportunities.

Setting and Using on the Ball Screens

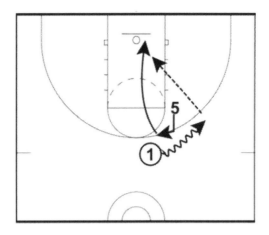

Defenses will often attempt to negate an effective on the ball screen by trapping the ball handler before the screen is set, or by "showing early help" with the screener's defender. One tactic to negate these ploys by the defense is for the screener to "slip" the screen and receive a pass for a lay-up as depicted in the diagram above. The screener approaches as normal to set the screen and when the defense reveals its tactic, "slips" to the rim while giving a directional hand target to the ball handler for purposes of clear communication.

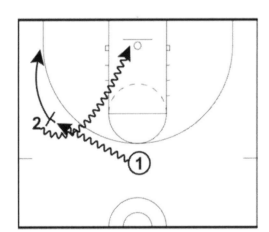 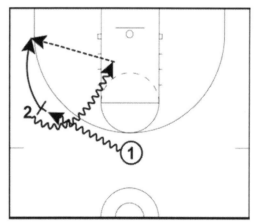

For those who like "old school" basketball, the dribble exchange from the days of "weave" offenses is an effective way to enter an offense against teams who play aggressive denial defense on guard to wing offensive entry passes. The ball handler drives at the player who is to be screened for, executes a jump stop in a good screening stance as close to the defender as possible. The cutter takes the ball in an exchange, rubs shoulders with the screener and drives. The screener rolls to an appropriate open area on the court. In the two examples shown above, the #2 drives for a lay-up in the first example and passes to the screener for an open shot in the second example.

The Fine Art of Cutting and Screening

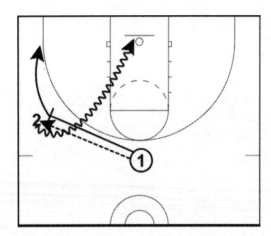 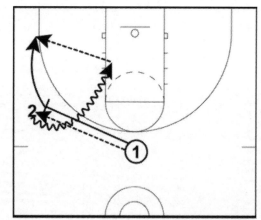

Another "old school" on ball screen entry to half court offense is the pass, follow and screen. This is a big departure from the several decades long standard of pass and screen away. The passer makes the entry pass and follows it, setting a screen on the new ball handler. The diagrams above depict two common outcomes.

Simple Drills to Teach Screening and Cutting

When selecting or creating drills to teach concepts always keep in mind the principle of skill (concept) specificity. Only use the drill if it fits the offensive system being utilized. If the drill does not teach the specific skills and fundamentals required for offensive success, do not use the drill. Adapt drills to be more game-like, or similar to how the players will actually run the offense in a game.

This can be as simple a spacing the drill so it best simulates the alignment of the offense or the players run the cuts and use the screen angles required for the offense to be executed in the most efficient manner possible.

Start with the most basic skills and build from the bottom up. Footwork is so overlooked and good footwork is essential for proper cutting and screening. The ability to turn (pivot) and maintain good body balance is essential as well.

When starting instruction, emphasize the small details of screening and cutting. Just teaching the details is not enough. Players do what their coaches emphasize, not what they teach.

Screeners must be tough individuals. When starting, use an air dummy from football to give the screener a small jolt when setting the screen. This will help the screener toughen up and learn to set hard screens and take the physical contact from aggressive defenders, preventing offensive fouls for illegal screens being called as well as retaliation fouls.

When introducing the combination of screening and cutting, do not allow them to score. Require perfect execution of every tiny detail, including the screener being a second cutter! This forces the players to pay attention to detail and "emphasizes" the importance of doing things right. When the players execute to the desired level, begin passing to the cutter for a shot. Have a second player or student assistant ready with an extra ball to pass to the screener, who is now a second cutter, for a shot.

Add defense to make the drills more game-like. Initially have the defense play at half speed to allow the offense to have some success. Then tell the defense to ramp up the intensity and go at game speed. Eventually make the drills competitive with a consequence for the losing players. This produces the most game-like atmosphere possible in practice situations.

The Fine Art of Cutting and Screening

Basic Movement Drills

UCLA Coach John Wooden thought the skills in these drills were so important he included them in every practice, regardless of the stage of the season. The skills covered in these drills include change of pace, v-cutting (change of direction), start steps, jump stops, pivots (turns), step lunges and can include defensive skills such as closeouts.

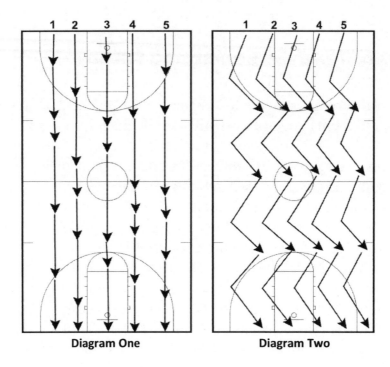

Diagram One   Diagram Two

    Diagram One depicts the basic alignment used for these drills. Lines of players can be formed across the baseline and the entire court utilized. If space is limited and large numbers of players must be accommodated, the lines can be moved to the sidelines instead. Groups of players as large as 20 to 25 can be accommodated on the baseline in most gyms. Each set of skills should be executed twice, meaning the players should make a trip down the court and back. *This is an excellent drill to use immediately at the start of practice to warm the muscles prior to stretching.*

    Diagram One also shows players executing "change of pace." Change of pace is a concept that actually requires a good deal of practice. Standing still, jogging, accelerating, decelerating and sprinting are all components of changing pace. Basketball players must master this simple, but not always easy, skill in order to be effective on offense. A key coaching point is to remind players this drill is neither a contest nor a race and standing still is one of the things they must do when executing this drill.

    Diagram Two depicts the players executing v-cuts en masse. Note, all of the players start by going to their right. This is to prevent injuries due to collision. Players enter the v-cut (change of direction) moving slowly, plant the foot opposite the direction they intend to cut towards, lower their hips, explode in the opposite direction and quickly raise their hands to provide an appropriate hand target for the passer. If players do not master this skill, they will not be able to properly utilize screens to get open in any offense.

Players move on their own, v-cutting as they move down the court. The next line starts when the preceding line is about 15 feet down the court. Players must "cover distance," meaning moving horizontally at least 15 to 17 feet, and the cut must be at an angle, not a curve. If the player does not cover 15 to 17 feet horizontally, the defense will have an easy time recovering and denying the cutter the ball. Cutting with a curve and not an angle does not produce a sharp, defined change in direction. This poor technique will also allow a defender to make an easy recover and deny a pass to an offensive player.

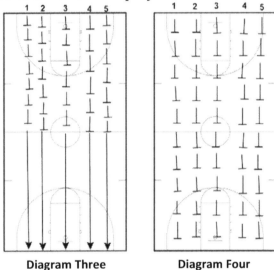

Diagram Three   Diagram Four

Diagram Three depicts players executing step lunges. While not a skill that will be used during a game, step lunges emphasize long, low steps and help players develop balance, flexibility and the long low and straight step required for either a direct drive or a crossover move. Players should have their hands up, palms out, elbows are extensions of their shoulders and the backs of the player's hands should be visible. This further enhances balance and helps to develop the proper hand positioning when a player is posting up. Once the players reach half court they jog to the other end of the court.

Start steps, jump stops (stops) and turns (pivots) are practiced as the last drill in the movement drill series and are depicted in **Diagram Four**. Players execute a long, low start step from a triple threat stance. Players may execute either a direct drive or a crossover step as indicated by the coach or simply decide for themselves which to practice.

Players execute a hop off the foot used to make the long, low start step. Players then execute a jump stop off the hop, making certain the hop is neither overly long

The Fine Art of Cutting and Screening

or high and both feet come in contact with the court at the same time, allowing for either foot to be used as a pivot foot. Players land softly and in a triple threat stance.

After landing, the player executes a turn or pivot. There are two basic types of turns that can be executed on either foot. A front turn, or pivot, is a turn made towards the front of the player. A rear turn is made towards the rear of the player. Turns can either be left or right footed.

A turn is executed by lifting the heel of the foot to be pivoted on. At the same time the player shifts slightly more weight to the pivot foot and uses the ball of the foot as the pivot point. The opposite leg is "whipped" around, providing the momentum to complete a 180-degree turn. The player must stay low through out the entire turn.

The key to this is for players to maintain a low, wide base while turning and to keep their head centered between the knees and the chin level. Standing up during a pivot is the worst mistake a player can make in executing a pivot as the player will turn slower and lose balance, requiring more time as the player returns to a good triple threat stance with a wide, low base of body support.

Players move down the court executing long, low start steps, jump-stops followed by turns. Of all the movement skills, this series is the most important. Once the preceding group has made two sets of starts, stops and turns the next group may begin.

Fundamental Lines

Fundamental lines is a series of drills designed to practice essential fundamentals, provide a high number of repetitions in a short period of time, build intensity and force players to concentrate on execution. The drills shown in this section can be run from the baseline, the ideal location, or the sideline if space and numbers dictate. Players ideally are in groups of three with a ball but groups of four or five are acceptable.

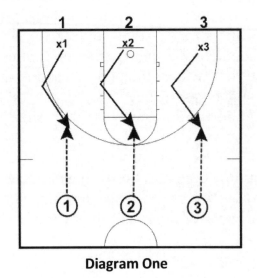

Diagram One

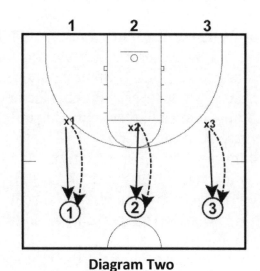

Diagram Two

Diagrams One and Two depict the drill sequence known as "easy running." This is drill is not meant to be performed at a high rate of speed and is a good warm-up for the more intense drills in this sequence. The first half of the sequence is shown in **Diagram One** as the players on the baseline execute v-cuts. The passers are located near half court and pass to the cutter using their weak hand. Upon catching the pass, the cutter lands in triple threat and executes a weak hand pass back to the passer.

The cutter follows the pass to the passer and executes a jump stop into triple threat and takes an exchange from the passer, who is in triple threat with the ball, by pulling the ball from the grasp of the passer and then executing a rear turn. The passer moves out of bounds and hustles to the end of the cutter line on the baseline (**Diagram Two**).

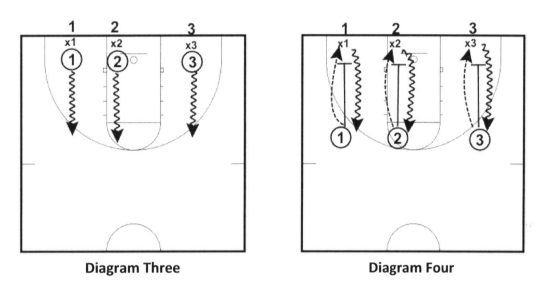

Diagram Three **Diagram Four**

The next sequence in fundamental lines is "live ball." Transition to this second sequence by verbally calling "live ball." The player with the ball in each group, at that time, passes the ball to the first player in line, follows the pass and closes-out on the ball.

Diagrams Three and Four depict how the live ball series works. The first player in line executes a two-inch up fake or pass fake and then executes a long, low, straight start step, either a direct drive or a crossover. The player is to travel as far as possible with two dribbles, jump stop and execute a rear turn (pivot) in triple threat position. The player then passes the ball to the next player in line using a weak hand pass.

The player receiving the pass steps to the pass to shorten the pass. A good measure for a player or coach to determine if this happens is for the receiving player to be out of bounds when the pass is made and to catch the ball inbounds. The receiver catches the ball in triple threat position with a low, wide, base of balance and support.

The Fine Art of Cutting and Screening

The passer follows the pass and executes a defensive closeout. The receiver then executes a live ball move and takes two dribbles, executes a rear turn and makes a weak hand pass back to the next player. The sequence continues until the players are told to progress to the next series.

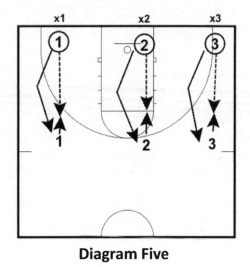
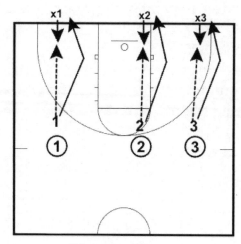

Diagram Five **Diagram Six**

Diagram Five depicts the start of the third, and most mentally challenging, phase of the fundamental lines series known as flick passing. Players transition from the live ball series by having a player execute the live ball move followed by two dribbles and pass the ball back to the first player on the baseline. This sequence must always start with the ball in the group of players with at least two players. The player who just executed the live ball move remains 15 to 18 feet away and awaits a return pass to start the sequence.

Following the transition from one drill to the next, the drill starts with the player with the ball on the baseline passing to the single player opposite. In the examples shown in **Diagrams Five and Six** the players are using a right hand pass to pass away from the defense.

All groups must start with the same pass. The passer follows the pass with a v-cut and a jump stop and rear turn behind the player who just received the ball. By starting the drill with all players using the same hand to pass with, collisions and injuries will be avoided.

The receiver must take a step to meet, or shorten, the pass. The receiver then repeats the procedure of the passer who initiated the drill. The drill continues until the coach gives the order to change hands being passed with. The drill continues without stopping, players simply change passing hands and the side to which players execute their v-cut. The key rule for players to remember for purposes of safety is to cut to the side of the hand the player passed with.

Four Line Lay-ups and Shooting Progression

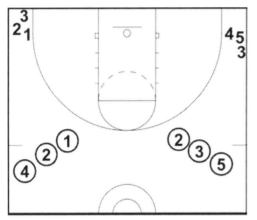

Basic alignment to run the four line drills.

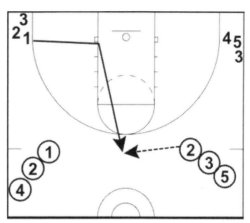

The initial cut to practice lay-ups obtained by driving against the grain.

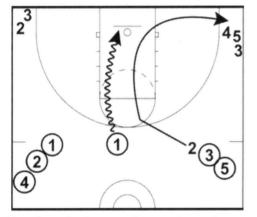

#2 makes a basket cut after passing and moves to the end of the line the corner. #1 shot fakes and drives against the grain before moving to the end of the line in the corner.

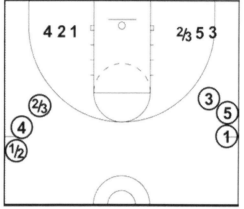

This diagram shows the adjusted starting point for high post lay-ups.

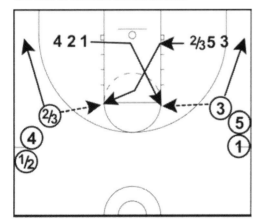

Both post lines execute v-cuts and flash into the high post. Different v-cuts are used to avoid collisions and practice take the defense low if playing low and high if playing high.

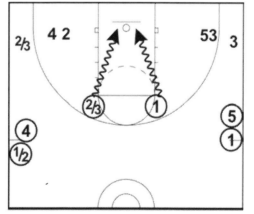

The passers cut to fill the corner areas. The high posts execute drop steps and drive for one bounce lay-ups, chinning the ball before shooting.

The Fine Art of Cutting and Screening

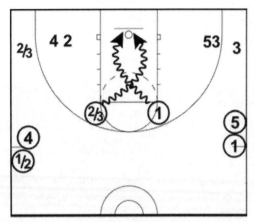

In this next stage of the progression of high Post lay-ups, the post players execute rear turns and drive across the lane to shoot lay-ups.

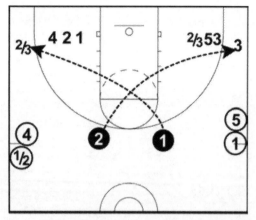

To make the drill more versatile, coaches or student assistants can make skip passes to the perimeter players who cut to the corners for 3-point shot attempts.

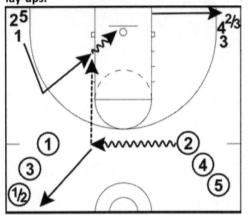

The next stage of the progression is backdoor lay-ups. Each side must alternate. Note the perimeter player drives across the lane to bounce pass down the lane line.

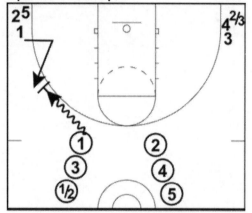

The dribble exchange is the next step in the progression. The perimeter player drives at the wing, jump stops/screens, and makes a hand off/exchange with the wing.

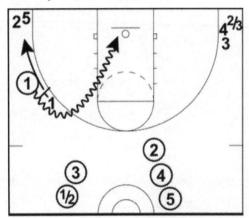

The wing drives the middle for a lay-up while the perimeter guard finishes the "pick" and roll.

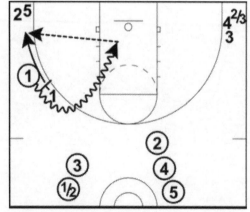

The guard passes to the screener for a shot. This screener is capable of shooting 3-point shots so the screener "rolls" to a 3-point shot location.

Simple Drills to Teach Screening and Cutting

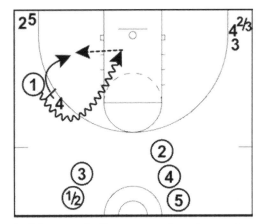

In this example the screener is not a good outside shooter so the screener cuts to a shot location in his/her range.

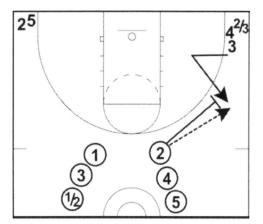

The next stage of the progression works on following the pass and screening.

The Fine Art of Cutting and Screening

Screening Progression

Successfully shooting of a screen requires good footwork, proper execution of screening and cutting techniques by two players, recognition by every player involved on offense, the ability to communicate with hand signals and finally the ability to shoot off the pass. The screening progression drill is designed to practice all of these essential skills at once.

The drill can be done with or without defense, though in the learning stages it is essential the offense have success and master the small details involved, requiring the defense to be absent from the drill. Defense may be added in stages, starting with token pressure and working up to game intensity.

The drill is a sequenced progression of screens and cuts, hence the name of the drill. The sequence is as follows: down screen, flare screen, back screen, pin screen and re-screen (**Diagrams A** through **D**).

The re-screen, setting a particular type of screen followed by the appropriate matching screen, for example, a down screen followed by a flare screen, can be changed each practice session. The cutter shoots each time after coming off the screen taking a total of five shots before rotating to be a passer, screener or rebounder as determined by the coach.

A variation of the drill is to use two passers, passing to the screener reinforcing the concept of being a second cutter. A Shoot-A-Way™ can be used as well to ease the process of running down missed shots and making certain the passers have enough balls to keep the screener and cutter moving at a constant pace.

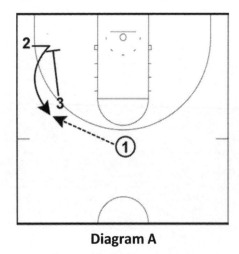

Diagram A

Diagram B

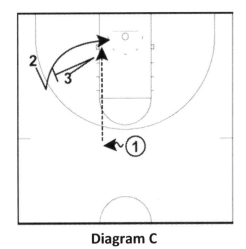

Diagram C   **Diagram D**

Lagniappe - Something Extra

The following material has been excerpted from *Fine Tuning Your Zone Attack Offense: 50 Concepts to Improve Your Team's Zone Attack Offense*.

Screen-in

Screening the zone is an effective yet seldom used tactic. The screen-in tactic is highly effective at setting up a three-point shot attempt and entering the ball into either the low post or high post. **Diagram A** depicts the initial alignment against the backline of a 2-3 zone. For clarity the top two defenders have been omitted from the diagrams.

The wing opposite the ball, #2, slides down behind the low post opposite the ball. The ball is skip passed by #3 to #2 in the corner while #5 sets a legal back screen on the last defender of the zone defense (**Diagram B**). If #2 has enough time, this will result in an excellent three-point shot opportunity.

When setting the back screen, not only does #5 have to give the defender being screened one step, the screen must be set at such an able the defender fights over the screen on the high side, or the side away from the baseline.

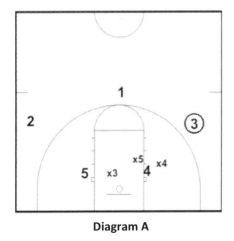

Diagram A

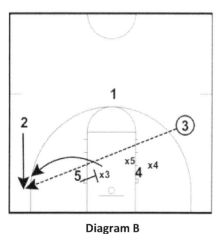

Diagram B

The reason for setting the screen at this angle is to create plenty of space for a baseline bounce pass to enter the ball into the low post.

After X3 fights over the screen from #5 and #5 goes to the next closest post defender and executes a rear turn (pivot) and seals the defender. The other offensive post player, #4, flashes into the ball side high post from behind the zone defense (**Diagram C**). If #5 is open in the low post #2 makes the entry pass for a scoring opportunity.

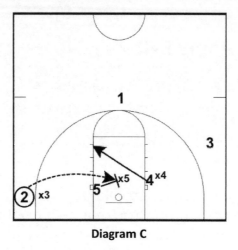

Diagram C

If the ball is entered into the high post #5 changes the angle of the post seal to set up for a high low pass. The defender still must be pinned in the middle of the lane in order to create both a passing lane and a shot after catching the ball (**Diagram D**).

Diagram D

Screen-out

The screen-out is a somewhat unorthodox tactic and must be executed carefully to avoid fouling, yet it can be highly effective. The set-up for a screen-out is shown in **Diagram A**.

The opposite post player #5 flashes into the high post and receives a pass from the wing #3. On the pass the offensive low post #4 steps out from the low post, rear turns (pivot) and seals the defender X3 who was pressuring the perimeter back to back. This "seal" creates space for a short bank shot just outside of the lane if executed properly.

Once X3 has been screened-out, #5 will be able to make a high low pass to #4 for a score (**Diagram B**).

Diagram A

The low post can shoot or look to pass. In **Diagram C** #4 fans the ball out to a three-point shooter #2 with a diagonal skip pass opposite. Another possible option would be for #5 to cut from the high post to the opposite low post block for a back half of a duck cut.

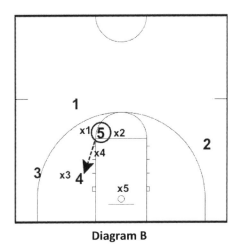

Diagram B

The Fine Art of Cutting and Screening

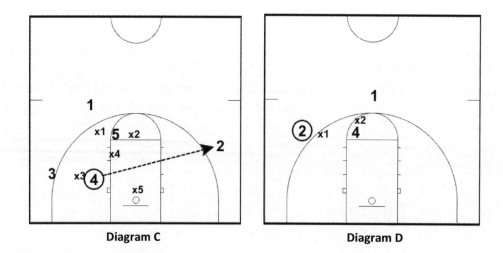

Diagram C   Diagram D

The screen out tactic can also be employed in the high post area (**Diagram D**). On the pass from #2 to the perimeter player on top of the three-point line #4 steps out and executes a rear turn and seals X1 back-to-back. X2 must move quickly to pressure the ball, creating a passing lane to #4 (**Diagram E**).

The post player can shoot, make a high low pass for a shot, drive or fan the ball to a perimeter player for a scoring opportunity.

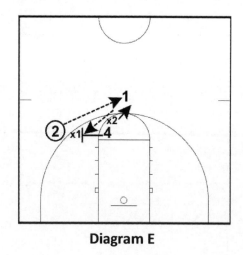

Diagram E

Screen Down

The screen down is very similar to setting a down screen against a man-to-man defense. The perimeter player at the top of the three-point line simply sets a down screen on the zone defender closest to the perimeter player opposite the ball. The perimeter player without the ball, #2, makes a v-cut to utilize the down and screen and receives the ball. The screener, #1, should balance the floor after setting the screen by filling what was #2's space on the court (**Diagram A**).

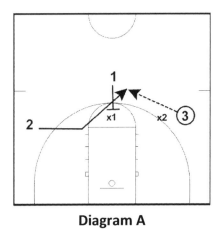

Diagram A

Flare Screen

Like the down screen, the flare screen is very similar as a flare screen set against man-to-man defense. Perimeter player #2 sets a flare screen on the last top zone defender X1. #1 makes a v-cut to utilize the flare screen, making certain his or her chest is facing the ball handler at all times.

#3 drives the flare screen to freeze the defender being screened by taking one or two dribbles and then skip passing the ball to the cutter for a three-point shot attempt (**Diagram A**).

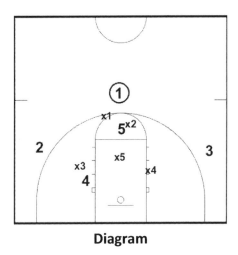

Diagram

Center Screen

The center screen tactic is designed to create an open shot in the low post area by screening the middle defender of the zone defense. **Diagrams A** and **B** depict the center screen tactic against a 2-1-2 zone. **Diagrams C** and **D** depict the center screen tactic against a 2-3 zone.

For this tactic to be effective the timing of the setting of the screen, the pass to the wing and the cut of the other post player must be carefully coordinated and timed.

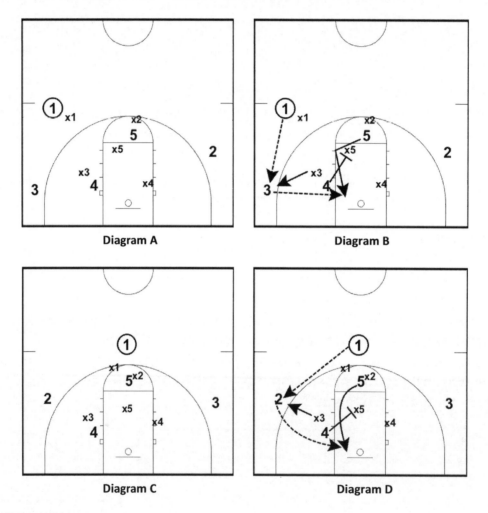

Diagram A

Diagram B

Diagram C

Diagram D

Combine Screens

As an offensive unit becomes more comfortable with the tactic of screening a zone defense, more and more screens should be used in combination against the zone. A screen-in could be set by a post player while a wing on the same side of the court sets a flare screen for a three-point shooter on the top of the three-point line.

This double screen may create a three-point shot or a great opportunity to enter the ball into the post for a score and possible foul (**Diagram A**).

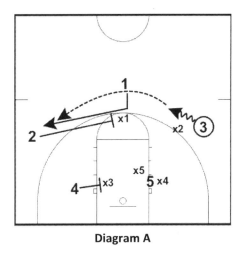

Diagram A

More Lagniappe!

The following material was excerpted from *Fine Tuning Your Man-to-Man Defense: 101 Concepts to Improve Your Team's Man-to-Man Defense*

Defending a Screen is a Two Defender Job

Defending a screen is a two-defender job at a minimum. Nothing is more demoralizing to a defender guarding a cutter than a help defender who simply does not provide help on the screen. The defender of a cutter who simply gives up and relies on the defender who is guarding the screener to handle the situation.

Defending any screening situation requires considerable effort and coordination between not just two, but all five defensive players.

Step Over and Fight Through Screens

Slipping under a screen or going over and around a screen is not effective defense. Slipping under the screen, while easier, sets the defender up to be re-screened for a flair screen or pinned down for a back screen, setting the cutter up for an excellent three-point shot or jump shot.

Simply following the cutter around the screen, particularly if the cutter utilizes a curl cut, is a recipe for an unguarded lay-up and is simply lazy defense.

Defense in general and man-to-man defense in particular requires a tough mental mind-set. The defender guarding the screener must use a verbal to not only warn the defender of the cutter that a screen is going to be set, but should provide some type of information as to where the screen will be set.

This warning allows the defender of the cutter to get into the cutter and prepare to defeat the screen. By getting into the cutter, the defender will have an easier time defeating the screen.

Defeating the screen requires the defender of the cutter to step over the screen. This technique allows the defender to cut in any direction necessary regardless of how the cutter uses the screen. By virtue of being halfway over the screen this tactic also defeats the very purpose of the screen itself, which is to completely impede the progress of the defender responsible for covering the cutter.

Once over the screen the defender of the cutter must chase the cutter's number/outside hip and arrive when the ball arrives for the cutter to catch the ball.

Protect the Rim on Screens Off the Ball

The defensive player guarding the screener has several responsibilities. The first is to verbally warn the defender of the cutter. The second is to "get wide early" and defend the rim (**Diagram 55-A**).

Diagram 55-A

Note in this example the help defender has gotten wide at the level of the screen being set. This is essential for the purpose of recovery as many offenses will use a screen to set up a shooter. The reason for X4 "getting wide" is to prevent any backdoor cuts being made by either the cutter or the screener. This is a highly effective tactic in preventing back door cuts and often results in steals against teams that utilize this offensive tactic off screens away from the ball. The defender executing this tactic only does so momentarily before returning to an appropriate defensive position.

By forcing the defender of the screener to give help, the screener now has an opening to step up to the ball for a catch and shoot opportunity (**Diagram 55-B**). By guarding the rim at the level of the ball, the defender responsible for the screener is able to recover and arrive when the ball arrives (**Diagram 55-C**).

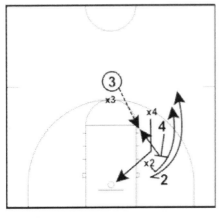

Diagram 55-B   **Diagram 55-C**

Number 56
Defending Double and Triple Screens

Defending double and triple staggered screens is a multiple defensive player effort requiring ball pressure to make any pass difficult, the goal to be protected, the cutter chased and space created for the defensive player of the cutter to fight over the screen.

As with any screening situation on defense, the first step is verbalize the screen. The defender of the cutter must get into the cutter and chase the outside hip The defender of the final screen in the staggered screen has gotten wide to protect the rim at the level of the final screen. The defender of the lowest screen moves close to create space. X3 has been omitted in this drawing for clarity (**Diagram 56-A**).

The Fine Art of Cutting and Screening

Diagram 56-A

A common triple staggered screen utilizes the low post player on the side of the court the cutter starts the cut from (**Diagram 56-B**). The only change in defensive responsibility is on the back screen set by #4, requiring X4 to open up and getting wide momentarily to defend the rim. After getting wide, X4 must quickly return to a denial position in order to prevent a quick entry pass into the offensive low post.

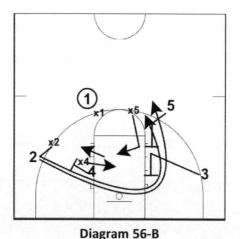

Diagram 56-B

Number 57
Defending Wall Screens

Defending wall screens requires the coordinated effort of a minimum of four defensive players: the on the ball defender pressuring the ball, the defender guarding the cutter, the defender of the top screen of the ball and the defender of the bottom screen of the wall.

The ball pressure makes the pass more difficult, buying time for the defensive player chasing the cutter and fighting through screens.

Lagniappe – Something Extra

The key defender in providing help in this scenario is the defensive player guarding the offensive player who sets the screen at the bottom of the wall screen (**Diagram 57-A**).

X2 has heeded the verbal warning a screen is going to be set and has gotten into the cutter and is chasing the outside hip. X3 has opened up and gotten wide at the level of the highest screen. X1 is pressuring the ball to make any pass as difficult as possible.

X5 has inserted his or her body in between the two screeners setting the wall screen. This accomplishes several key tactics. First, in the unfortunate event X2 is unable to fight through the first part of the screen, X5 will be able to momentarily arrive when the ball arrives, as the closest defender, buying X2 more time and denying the offensive player a quick shot.

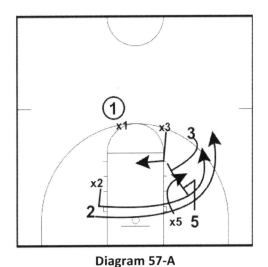

Diagram 57-A

It also allows X5 to quickly dead front #5 should the offense attempt to quickly post up #5 (**Diagram 57-B**). Other players omitted for clarity.

Diagram 57-B

Number 58
Defending Post-to-Post Screens

Defending post-to-post screens is one of the most difficult screens to defend and requires excellent coordination between the two defenders involved. Two different post-to-post screening scenarios have been depicted.

Diagram 58-A

In **Diagram 58-A** a low post to low post screen is depicted. X4 has opened up to get wide and protect the rim (*Number 55*). X5 has gotten into the cutter and chased around the screen set by #4. The reality of this scenario is X4 is defending the rim against a cut to the offensive low post by #5 until X5 can arrive. Then X4 must quickly reposition to prevent a quick pass over to #4 for an easy score.

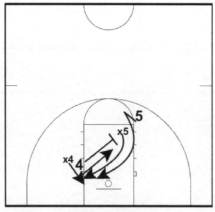
Diagram 58-B

In **Diagram 58-B** a low post to high post screen is depicted. X4 again opens up to protect the rim while X5 follows all the rules of defending a cutter. As soon as X5 has beaten #5 to the spot in the low post, releasing X4 to reposition to prevent #4 from being open for an easy pass.

Lagniappe – Something Extra

Number 59
Trap Ball Screens

Trapping ball screens is an effective method of negating ball screens. For this tactic to be effective, it must be executed with assertiveness and no hesitation by the two defensive players executing the trap and depending on the scouting report on the offense, a third defensive player may be needed to rotate to cover the screener if the offense responds to the trap by slipping the screener for a quick pass and scoring opportunity.

In **Diagram 59-A** the offense is setting a screen on the ball on the wing. As soon as X5 realizes #5 is going to set a ball screen X5 warns X1 with a verbal for a ball screen and immediately begins to provide early help in the form of a trap on the ball handler. X1 still gets into the cutter and X5 arrives before the screener does. The trap must be set before the screen arrives and all angles of escape via the dribble taken away.

Diagram 59-A

Number 60
Show on Ball Screens

Defending ball screens without trapping the ball can be done effectively by "showing" early on the ball screen with early help from the defensive player guarding the screener (**Diagram 60-A**).

X3 recognizes #3 is going to set a ball screen for #1 and calls the verbal "ball screen right." X3 immediately "turns the corner" and plays at a right angle to X1 BEFORE #3 can arrive to set the screen. This tactic resembles a trap and encourages #1 to dribble wide and around the "show" by X3. On hearing the verbal warning a ball screen is coming, X1 should have "gotten into" the cutter and can skinny up and fight over #3's ball screen if #1 has not already left to avoid the apparent trap.

X3 only shows long enough to force #1 wide then recovers to a denial position on #3. X1 must recover to proper on the ball positioning as quickly as possible. X3 must also take care to not impeded X1's recovery to on the ball defense, granting X1 the clearest path to #1.

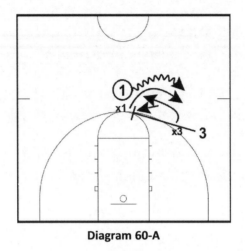

Diagram 60-A

Make the Ball Handler Pick Up the Dribble on a Ball Screen

The pick and roll has long been a staple in the game of basketball, particularly in the NBA. In recent years it has enjoyed resurgence in the college and high school game. It is an effective offensive tactic, forcing the defense to react to a screen and to cover a cutter.

One of the best strategies to defend the pick and roll is to proactively force the ball handler to pick up the dribble. This eliminates the threat of dribble penetration, allowing the on the ball defender to pressure the ball without fear. The defender of the screener can now totally focus on covering the cut, usually to the goal, being made by the screener.

There are several methods that can be used to encourage the ball handler to pick up the dribble. The easiest is to simply have both the on the ball defender and the screener's defender trap the ball handler. This method will require that a third teammate cover the screener/cutter.

A second method requires the defender of the screener to show help early, possibly faking a trap, to discourage the use of the screen. With this method, the object is to encourage the ball handler to believe a trap is coming or that the second defender has committed, leaving the screener open to slip the screen for a pass.

For this method to be successful, the second defender must be adept at both faking the trap/showing early help, and anticipating the s lip screen by the screener. If the second defender can take away the pass on the slipped screen, the ball handler has no immediate passing opportunity and the pick and roll has been defeated.

The third method is the most difficult but is the safest. The second defender calls screen to alert the on the ball defender to the fact that a pick and roll screen is about to be set. The on the ball defender "gets into the ball handler" by getting as close as possible.

As the screener approaches, the second defender shows early help in an effort to cause the ball handler to hesitate. The on the ball defender "skinnies up" by stepping through and over the screener, using both a leg and an arm to establish position in a gap between the ball handler and the screener. This tactic neutralizes the screen and will force the ball handler to drive in a wider than desired path.

By crowding the ball handler through the screen and forcing the dribble penetration into a wider than desired path, it is hoped that the ball handler will pick up the dribble. The second defender recovers to a denial position as quickly as possible, preventing a pass to the screener/cutter.

Despite the difficulty of this method, it is the safest as the screener/cutter is always covered and there is no need for a third defensive player to rotate to cover an open cutter.

About the Author

A 25 year veteran of the coaching profession, with twenty-two of those years spent as a varsity head coach, Coach Kevin Sivils amassed 464 wins and his TEAMs earned berths in the state play-offs 19 out of 22 seasons with his TEAMs advancing to the state semi-finals three times. An eight time Coach of the Year Award winner, Coach Sivils has traveled as far as the Central African Republic to conduct coaching clinics. Coach Sivils first coaching stint was as an assistant coach for his college alma mater, Greenville College, located in Greenville, Illinois.

Coach Sivils holds a BA with a major in physical education and a minor in social studies from Greenville College and a MS in Kinesiology with a specialization in Sport Psychology from Louisiana State University. He also holds a Sport Management certification from the United States Sports Academy.

In addition to being a basketball coach, Coach Sivils is a classroom instructor and has taught U.S. Government, U.S. History, the History of WW II, and Physical Education and has won awards for excellence in teaching and Teacher of the Year. He has served as an Athletic Director and Assistant Athletic Director and has also been involved in numerous professional athletic organizations.

Sivils is married to the former Lisa Green of Jackson, Michigan, and the happy couple are the proud parents of three children, Danny, Katie, and Emily. Rounding out the Sivils family are three dogs, Angel, Berkeley, and Al. A native of Louisiana, Coach Sivils currently resides in the Great State of Texas.

To Contact the Author

If you have any questions about the content of **The Art of Cutting and Screening** or any of my other books, please feel free to contact me! I can be contacted by e-mail at:

info@kcsbasketball.com

To sign-up for my FREE e-Newsletter, **The Roundball Report**, please visit my website CoachSivils.com and register for the newsletter.

Website

To visit my website please go to www.CoachSivils.com or www.kcsbasketball.com

Blogs

To visit my blog about basketball, **The Basketball Coach's Notebook**, go to http://www.kcsbasketball.com/blog/

To visit my blog about the mental side of sports, **Teach to Win**!, go to www.teachtowin.com

Twitter

To follow on Twitter please go to *https://twitter.com/#!/CoachSivils*

Facebook

To follow on Facebook please go to *http://www.facebook.com/CoachSivils?sk=wall*

Please be sure to "Like" the page!

Amazon Store

Please visit the Amazon Store at CoachSivils.com.

The Lady Mustangs

I want to thank the four young ladies whose willing sacrifice of time made much of this book possible. During the four years our two seniors played the Lady Mustangs won over 100 varsity games, qualifying for the State Play-offs each of the four seasons!

The Senior Captains – Class of 2012

Kandis Harding No. 12

Kaitlyn HIrschbuehler No. 11

The Juniors – Class of 2013

Miranda Rogers No. 22*

Ashton Binkley No. 1

*First Team All State Class 5-A 2011-12

Other Books in the Fine Tuning Series:

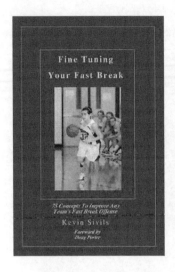

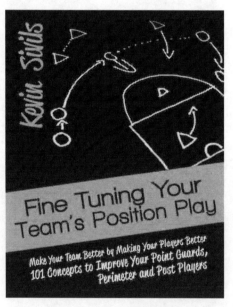

Available from Amazon, Barnes and Noble and Syskos Sports

Printed in Poland
by Amazon Fulfillment
Poland Sp. z o.o., Wrocław